Liberosis

Sunakshi Singla

BookLeaf Publishing

India | USA | UK

Made with ❤ on the BookLeaf Publishing Platform
www.bookleafpub.in
www.bookleafpub.com

Dedication

'Life is a beautiful mess'

Jake Peralta, Season 2, Episode 22

Preface

Hey! This is a piece of my heart, and here's why I'm sharing it with you.

These pages are for anyone who has ever felt like an echo, or like a heartbeat slightly out of sync with the rest of the world. These poems are small places to settle down in, to breathe. Some of them came to life on gentle days, and others showed up when nothing felt right, but they're all pieces of what it feels like to grow up and wonder if you'll ever feel whole.

This book contains few poems, some longer than others, all written for those who feel like they have too many thoughts and not enough words. It's a book that grew slowly, poem by poem, out of a weird combination of teenage angst and an insane amount of caffeine.

If you've ever had a staring contest with the ceiling at 3 a.m., questioned every life choice after dropping your phone on your face—then you'll feel right at home here.

I hope these poems remind you, that no matter what you're going through, you're definitely not alone. It's not always easy, but it's a lot less lonely when you realize we're all just learning, messing up, and trying again.

I hope this book finds you exactly when you need it
most, and maybe—even just a little—it changes your life.

Acknowledgements

They say no journey is walked alone, and while that sounds poetic, I can promise you it's also true. Behind every page in this book are people who've laughed with me, believed in me, and occasionally reminded me to get some sleep. This book is, *in a way*, theirs as much as mine.

To my family, for providing a solid foundation, a roof over my head, an unlimited supply of chai, and—most importantly—the DNA that made me this stubborn, creative, and a bit of a dreamer. For every eye roll, patience, and push to keep going, thank you. (especially to my dad) Your support (even if you only partly understood this whole poetry thing) means the world. To my mom, my superhero, my rock—thank you for being the unwavering strength in my life, even when it gets messy. You may be the reason I fight hard, but you're also the reason I stand strong. Your support means the world.

To my unofficial editors—Hitesh and Unnathi—my truest late-night lifesavers. You are the ones who turned this dream into reality, page by page. Thank you for listening to my terrible first drafts, for hyping me up even when

my confidence wobbled, and for keeping my head out of
the clouds. You are the laughter behind these lines and
the extra push on the hardest days. This book exists
because of you, because you showed up every time.
I would also like to specially mention Anshul and Ved,
who have seen every version of me—flawed, funny, and
probably a little too dramatic at times—and yet,
somehow, they stayed. Thank you for your constant
inspiration and, most importantly, for never sugar-
coating anything (even when I really wanted you to).
Your honesty is the kind of brutal I never knew I needed.

Last but definitely not the least,
I would like to thank my English teacher, Dr. Hussaina.
You were the one who pushed me to share my words
with the world and opened the door that led me here.
Your belief in my poetry gave me the courage to step
forward, and your guidance was the spark that turned
this dream into reality.

*This book holds pieces of you all, woven into every
word.*

1. amalgamation

I don't really know who I am,
I guess no one does,
Who has the answer to life's big question:
Who are you? Who am I?

I've worn a mask for so long I forgot it was there,
I diluted my problems because they were always too
much
My façade felt like my face, not someone else's
And now when I try to take it off,
I realise I dont know a single true thing about myself.

I've always fitted in with those around me,
adopted mannerisms and phrases
I became an amalgamation of everyone I admired,
I slotted bits and pieces into my personality like I was a
jigsaw puzzle,
But they were all stolen, and not the right size.

2. affinity

I have recently realized the importance of friends;
like I always knew it, but now it makes sense—
that life was never meant to be lived alone,
but with a shoulder to cry on
and a hand to hold.
I have recently realized that life is so much better
if you learn to choose your friends wisely.
Then life
may not always be so grimy.
I don't know what it is,
but it is pretty special.
It's like a warm bath for a strained muscle—
the way we slide into the water,
knowing that the world is still there,
knowing that it will ache again,
knowing that we will survive.

3. unbecoming

Life sometimes feels like sitting on the floor of your
mom's bedroom at 8 years old wondering why the kids
at school don't like you,
It feels like 6th grade, when the kids in class wouldn't
allow you in their group,
Its that same pit in your stomach, all over again,
the same wondering feeling,
about why you weren't enough,
why you can't just be someone people want to be
around,
wondering constantly what you could've done to save
something that is no longer yours.
I thought I would outgrow crying in the arms of my
mother,
tears shed all over her fav pyjamas,
but as I grow, my problems grow with me.
I have spent so much time trying to feel accepted,
protected and unaffected.
So much time pretending to be her,
learning to be her,
becoming her,
that I forgot to become me.

4. suffuse

Sometimes it all feels a little too tight,
like the worlds closing in, and nothings quite right.
Even in the spaces where I'm meant to be,
It all turns heavy, and something feels wrong.

The walls start to close, the air's too thin,
and panic rises slowly, from somewhere within.
I'm in my element, I should be fine,
But suddenly, I'm losing the rhythm,
blurring the lines.

I try to breathe, to push it away,
But the fear takes over, and I start to sway.
In a room full of light, I'm lost in the dark,
trying to find some peace, trying to regain the spark.

5. veins

Sticks and stones may break my bones,
But words will break my confidence,
Words will break my trust,
Words will take who I am and make it who I was.

They linger, those words, long after they're spoken,
Invisible wounds, pieces shattered and broken.
They cut deeper than anything seen,
A silent bruise that colours where I've been.

Actions leave scars, but they fade in time,
While words echo on, like a haunting rhyme.
They twist and they turn, reshaping me still,
Taking parts of myself against my will.

It's strange, the weight a few words can hold—
How they burrow beneath, how they cling, take control.
Sticks and stones may leave me bruised,
But words, they're a pain I can't ever lose.

6. inadequacy

I never feel enough, no matter what I try,
Like I'm chasing something that's always passing by.
The world keeps moving, and I'm stuck in place,
Falling behind in this endless race.

I watch others succeed, like it's so easy to do,
While I'm left wondering what's wrong with me, too.
I work, I push, but it's never quite right,
Always a step behind, out of sight.

And maybe it's me, maybe I'm just slow,
Maybe I'm missing something I should know.
But the weight of it all is heavy and real,
This constant doubt, this sinking feel.

I try to keep up, but it's never enough,
No matter how much I give, life's always too tough.
And I wonder if one day, I'll finally see,
What it's like to be enough, to just be me.

7. ashes

There's a quiet comfort in the burn,
a heat that melts the cold,
a flame that dances against my skin
like a secret, softly told.

But when the light fades,
and the warmth is gone,
I'm left with the echo,
the quiet that lingers on.

8. confusion

Me. Who am I?
Such a small question yet it leaves me speechless,
I want to answer honestly—
But I have fabricated such an image that everything
seems like a lie,
but I am learning.
Learning that the only acceptance I need is mine,
That I can protect myself by saying no,
And letting the idea that I need to be a hero go.
I'm learning to be me,
Slowly, scared and steadily,

9. blueprints

They say actions speak louder than words,
but what about the words we never say?
Are we made of quiet thoughts,
the ones that live behind our ribs,
or the things we do in daylight,
the messy fingerprints we leave behind?
Thoughts are the blueprints, maybe,
and actions are the bricks we lay,
but there's a gap between dreaming and doing—
a place where intentions get lost,
where we wonder if who we want to be
is someone we can become.
Maybe we're both:
the quiet and the noise, the hope and the hands,
a map still written in pencil,
searching for a place where thoughts and actions
finally feel like one.

10. indifference

They say the opposite of love isn't hate,
it's indifference.
But no one warns you how easy it is to slip
from love to less than that,
how caring starts to feel like wearing shoes that don't
quite fit—
you'll keep walking, sure,
but your heels are already bleeding.
Somewhere between "How was your day?"
and "I knew you'd say that,"
I became, a muted echo,
the kind you hear through walls but can't make out the
words.
It's like I forgot what full sentences feel like,
how to occupy my own mouth with something real,
something *whole*
instead of just "I'm fine."
Maybe one day I'll remember how it felt to care,
and it won't feel like wearing shoes that are two sizes
too small.
Maybe one day, I'll take a deep breath,
and my chest won't feel like it's sinking.
Until then, I'll be here,
practicing indifference

like it's an art form I'm still trying to learn,
like it's a coat that I know doesn't fit,
but, I wear it, still,—because it's all I have left.

11. apathy

I've been the second opinion for so long,
I wonder if I was ever the first.
Did I ever own the space between breaths,
the moments before the yes, or was I always the maybe,
the standby, the 'just in case'?

Being the second choice means you know how to wait,
but not how to hope.
And now, I don't want to care, not really,
because caring feels like opening a door
and watching it swing back shut—
no one else on the other side,
just you and the hollow click of metal,
just you, wondering if you heard it right.
Wondering when your heart forgot to ache.

12. echoes

They say freedom is the open road,
the wide, uncharted map with no one waiting,
no one holding you back.
But when there's no voice calling you home,
no light in the window at 2 a.m.,
is it freedom—or something else?

When you can do whatever you want,
move through the day like a breeze,
but there's no one beside you
to see—
is it freedom, or just space
that starts to feel like silence?

Maybe we're meant to have both:
to stand tall, to walk alone,
but still have someone there
to notice we're not always okay
in the quiet of the day.

13. serein

Is it bad to be soft, to feel every pain,
To carry the weight of others' rain?
Is it wrong to be gentle, when the world is so rough,
To offer your heart when it's never enough?

They tell me I'm fragile, that softness is weak,
That empathy breaks me, leaves me too meek,
But I wonder, is it truly a curse to care,
To notice the cracks when no one else dares?

Is it bad to be soft, when hardness surrounds,
To listen for whispers in a world full of sounds?
To reach out a hand when others would turn,
To soothe a fire when others watch it burn?

For in my softness, I see what they miss,
The quiet sorrow, the untold abyss.

14. inertia

Somewhere between the chaos
and the quiet,
there's this space that feels
too big,
too small,
too tight.

If I keep reaching,
will I ever catch the light?
Or am I running forever
from day to night?

Will I breathe through the mess,
or let it consume me whole,
will it swallow my thoughts,
and suffocate my soul?

is time something I own?
or does it own me

15. resonance

Thirteen years of the same old fight,
And every morning feels like night.

I don't ask for much—just quiet, you know?
But instead, I'm left to hear them go,
Back and forth, like how the waves flow,
Until I can't breathe and everything starts to slow.

I try to keep up, I try to stay strong,
But their yelling is louder than all my songs.
I'm busy, I'm tired, I'm just trying to get through,
And every shout feels like it's aimed at me too.

They don't see it—how much it weighs—
How it drags me down, how it steals my days.
I can't fix them, I can't make it stop,
But I'm tired of this world that keeps spinning nonstop.

So I keep my head down, I hold my ground,
Waiting for the silence that never comes around.
I don't need an apology, or a fix for the fight,
I just need a moment where I can breathe alright.

16. veiled

I wear a smile that doesn't quite fit,
A borrowed thing, so I don't have to admit
That inside, I'm slipping, drifting away,
Lost for words when they ask if I'm okay.

It's easier to nod, to say I'm fine,
To hide the cracks, to hold the line.
They want the version they know, the one who's strong,
So I play the part, just carry along.

But beneath the calm, there's a storm I can't share,
A heaviness I'm not ready to bear.
So I laugh and I nod, keep the questions at bay,
While I hope they don't see through the mask I display.

17. displaced dimples

Each day, the tide is rising fast,
a sea of tasks that hold me vast.
I swim through waves of "must" and "should,"
struggling to stay where I once stood.

Time slips away like sand through hands,
an endless stretch of unmet plans.
I gasp for air, but the waves don't cease—
just one moment of calm, one taste of peace.

Caught in currents I can't outrun,
chasing shorelines that blur and shun—
all I want is solid ground,
a place where I won't feel so drowned.

18. masquerade

I wear a smile that doesn't quite fit,
A borrowed thing, so I don't have to admit
That inside, I'm slipping, drifting away,
Lost for words when they ask if I'm okay.

It's easier to nod, to say I'm fine,
To hide the cracks, to hold the line.
They want the version they know, the one who's strong,
So I play the part, just carry along.

But beneath the calm, there's a storm I can't share,
A heaviness I'm not ready to bear.
So I laugh and I nod, keep the questions at bay,
While I hope they don't see through the mask I display.

19. reciprocity

To love or to be loved—is one more real?
To give of yourself, or to let yourself feel
The warmth of a care that's aimed at you,
A steady light, or a sky of blue.

To love is to reach, to open, to fall,
To give up pieces, to give it your all.
To be loved is softer, like drifting to shore,
A gentle comfort you don't need to implore.

But maybe they're tangled, these two things we seek,
Bound by the need to be brave or be weak.
For to love is to hope, to be loved is to trust—
Two sides of a coin, spun up from the dust.

20. displaced dimples

I once heard you laugh, and the world froze in place
You said your dimples dance all over your face,
But to me,
they're like paths that lead to your glow,
Guiding me gently wherever you go.
Each smile you share is a sun on the rise,
With dimples like stars that light up the skies
You think they stray, but they simply reveal,
The way that your heart makes everything real.
Your smile is the dawn that brightens my day.
And those dimples you fret are lost in the fray,
They are sunbeams that break through the clouds when you grin,
They are my favourite part of your grin.

21. haven

There's a quiet that settles,
a softness,
a calm,
when I'm wrapped in your arms,

It's the warmth of a heartbeat,
steady and near,
the kind of closeness
that melts every fear.

In that hold, I'm weightless,
floating, free—
like nothing could harm me,
like I'm finally me.

The world fades away,
its chaos unwinds,
and I'm left with the stillness
your hug leaves behind.

Liberosis

Liberosis is the art of letting go,
of loosening your grip on everything you think you
should be.
It's the quiet rebellion of caring less,
of not always glancing over your shoulder
to see who's watching,
who's judging,
who's waiting for you to stumble.
It's the freedom to be messy,
to love wildly,
to fail without apology.
To let life slip through your fingers
like water,
knowing you don't have to hold it all.
You just have to let it be.
And maybe,
just maybe,
you'll find peace in the letting go.

www.ingramcontent.com/pod-product-compliance
Lightning Source LLC
Chambersburg PA
CBHW071242140726
47996CB00007B/2717